The Wit of
Oscar Wilde

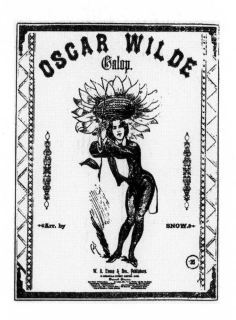

For Siobhan, Sean, Oonagh and Colum

The Wit of
Oscar Wilde

Sean McCann

THE O'BRIEN PRESS
DUBLIN

This edition first published 2008 by The O'Brien Press Ltd
12 Terenure Road East, Dublin 6, Ireland.
Tel: +353 1 4923333; Fax: +353 1 4922777
First published in paperback by The O'Brien Press Ltd, 1991.
Reprinted 1993, 1998, 2001, 2004.
E-mail: books@obrien.ie
Website: www.obrien.ie
Reprinted 2010.

Originally published 1969 in hardback by Leslie Frewin Publishers
Ltd., 15 Hays Mews, Berkely Square, London W1

ISBN: 978-1-84717-067-5

Text © copyright Sean McCann
Copyright for typesetting, layout, editing, design, illustrations
© The O'Brien Press Ltd

7 8 9 10 11 12
10 11 12

British Library Cataloguing-in-publication Data
Wilde, Oscar, 1854-1900
The wit of Oscar Wilde. - 6th ed.
1. Wilde, Oscar, 1854-1900 - Quotations
I. Title II. McCann, Sean
828.8'02

Layout and design: The O'Brien Press Ltd
Printed and bound by ScandBook AB, Sweden.
The paper in this book is produced using pulp from managed forests.

Picture credits: p. 1, reproduction of an American song cover, p. 3,
cartoon, Max Beerbohm

CONTENTS

Introduction

'My name,' he once said, 'has two O's, two F's and two W's. A name which is destined to be in everybody's mouth must not be too long. It comes so expensive in the advertisements. When one is unknown, a number of Christian names are useful, perhaps needful. As one becomes famous, one sheds some of them, just as a balloonist, when rising higher, sheds unnecessary ballast ... all but two of my five names have already been thrown overboard. Soon I shall discard another and be known simply as "The Wilde" or "The Oscar".'

The surprising thing about Oscar Fingal O'Flahertie Wills Wilde is not that he turned out to be one of the world's most tragic geniuses, but that things weren't a lot worse.

From the day in October 1854 when he was born

into the rare and slightly whacky atmosphere of a house on the south side of Dublin city the world was set to make him a spectacle.

His life could easily have been overawed by an extraordinary brace of parents. His father, Sir William Wilde, was one of Dublin's many great characters ... an auralist, an archaeologist and a surgeon; a man who was never really drunk but seldom sober; a man who liked 'other' women. His mother, renowned for her vitriolic verse and neurotic nationalism, was the product of a conservative Protestant family; an accomplished talker, untidy housewife and brilliant hostess. Pity any child born to this match. As it was, Oscar was the second – William Charles Kingsbury Wills Wilde arrived a year after the marriage and two years before Oscar. And when he came Oscar was a great disappointment to his mother ... she had her heart set on a daughter. But to make up for this genetic mistake she decided to let Oscar's hair grow into curls and ringlets and then dressed him in all the frills and flounces she would have lavished on a daughter. This lasted until he was nine years old.

His mother could not have held out much longer, for Oscar was growing tall and wide and when he was seventeen he was over six foot. He moved from his private school to Trinity College, Dublin, and from there to Oxford ... that was the beginning of the legend. Oscar became the 'Professor of Aesthetics', the cult of the day. He designed his own aesthetic costume – a loose shirt with turn-down collar and a large tie, usually green, done up in a great knot. He was the original flower child, professing a liking for large, spectacular poppies, lilies and sunflowers. He was ridiculed, jeered at, laughed at and cartooned. Even the stage had a go at him – once in *The Colonel*, a play written by the then editor of *Punch*, and again in Gilbert and Sullivan's *Patience*. Instead of causing Oscar's downfall, as many hoped, it was this stage mocking that made him.

To make sure that the American production of *Patience* would be a success it was decided to send Oscar on a lecture tour ... the subject being the principles of aestheticism ... the intention being to promote the show. In 1882 Oscar arrived in New York with 'nothing to declare but my genius'. And America laughed right away. He played everywhere, talking to cowboys, miners and screaming mobs of women. He told the world that, while in America, he had to hire two secretaries, 'one to write my autograph and answer the hundreds of letters that come begging for it; another, whose hair is brown, to send locks of his own hair to the ladies who write asking for mine. He is rapidly becoming bald.' Though he lectured in his aesthetic attire he refused to carry either a poppy or a sunflower. Before the tour was over he had become more a man of the wild west than the cowboys who lived there, eventually adopting the kneeboots, kerchief and ten-gallon hat of the cowboy. He was a riot wherever he went and arrived back in England more famous and more wanted by the hostesses of the day than when he left. No doubt this American tour was the making of Oscar.

He set about telling the world all about its pains and aches, its loves and wars, in a way that no one really mastered before. He assured his listeners that most people die of 'creeping common sense' ... and went off his own brilliant way ... a way that was a blend of kindness, willingness and deliberate art, mixed now and then with a liberal helping of verbal karate. He never suffered fools gladly but often made very sensible men seem foolish, especially when they tried to cross swords with him. This happened to Shaw, Whistler and especially Frank Harris.

On one famous occasion when Wilde, Max Beerbohm, Aubrey Beardsley, Rothenstein and Robert Ross were Harris's guests the host began to tell a long and detailed story which turned out to be a paraphrase of one of Anatole France's tales.

'What a charming story, Frank,' said Oscar, and then, after a pause, 'Anatole France would have spoiled it.'

Harris failed to see the irony and went on to talk of all the famous houses he had dined in throughout London. It was too much for Oscar, who bitingly commented:

'Yes, dear Frank, we believe you – you have dined in every house in London, once.'

His brand of repartee had no equal. One occasion when he was called upon to uphold his boast that he could talk spontaneously on any subject, the cry went up from a group of people:

'The Queen. Talk about the Queen.'

With hardly time for a pause Wilde replied:

'The Queen is not a subject.'

On another occasion when he was craving for a smoke but could not light up because the ladies had not left the room, a table lamp near him began to smoke. The hostess turned to him:

'Please put it out, Mr Wilde. It's smoking.'

'Happy lamp,' replied Oscar.

At a wedding when Lord Morris, who was renowned for his very thick Irish accent, was looking for a shoe to throw after the bridal couple, Oscar suggested:

'Why not throw your own brogue?'

His wit and humour were so much part of his make-up that he could keep an audience enthralled for hours ... he was a great mixture of the profound and the witty. Most of his sayings have gone round and round so often that even today they are being used as 'originals'. Very likely Wilde's own reaction to this would have been the one he used to a man who had just given a very honest summary of his religious beliefs:

'You are so evidently, so unmistakably, sincere, and most of all so truthful, that I can't believe a single word you say.'

Oscar knew everything, met everyone, could talk about men, women, children, books and every subject from sport to food. But he wasn't always ready to discuss them with everyman. He once greeted a guest with:

'Oh, I'm so glad you've come. There are a hundred

things I want not to say to you.'

He once said that nothing ages like happiness and certainly his own happiness aged quickly. Long before the end of his great career it was being whispered around London that he was a homosexual and on this charge he was convicted in 1895. It was the great tragedy of his life; he was not made for the harsh life of two years' hard labour in a nineteenth-century English prison. When he was released he moved to Paris and died there on 30th November 1900. He dictated a long letter to his friend Robert Ross on his deathbed in which he said:

'My throat is like a limekiln, my brain a furnace and my nerves a coil of angry adders. I am, apparently, in much the same state as yourself.'

In another context he said:

'I am dying, as I have lived, beyond my means.'

Despite this he left a legacy that is unlikely ever to be forgotten; a legacy of plays, poetry, criticism – but none more so than his ability as a wit. This collection cannot hope to present all his brilliant epigrams and witticisms; it does, however, show the importance of being Oscar ...

SEAN McCANN

Himself and Others

Wilde, asked what was his real ambition in life, replied:

God knows! I won't be a dried-up Oxford don, anyhow. I'll be a poet, a writer, a dramatist. Somehow or other I'll be famous, and if not famous I'll be notorious. Or perhaps ... I'll rest and do nothing .... These things are on the knees of the gods. What will be, will be.

It is sad. One half of the world does not believe in God, and the other half does not believe in me.

When I had to fill in a census paper I gave my age as nineteen, my profession as genius, my infirmity as talent.

When he heard a passer-by say: 'There goes that bloody fool Oscar Wilde', he remarked to his companion:

It's extraordinary how soon one gets known in London.

Wilde himself did not 'walk down Piccadilly with a poppy or a lily in his mediaeval hand', as Gilbert suggested in Patience. *Said Wilde long afterwards:*

Anyone could have done that. The great and difficult thing was what I achieved – to make the whole world believe that I had done it.

Going into a florist's shop in Jermyn Street, he asked for several bunches of flowers to be removed from the window. 'With pleasure, sir. How many would you like to have?' asked the assistant.

Oh, I don't want any, thank you. I only asked to have them removed from the window because I thought that they looked tired.

When people agree with me I always feel that I must be wrong.

I consider ugliness a kind of malady, and illness and suffering always inspire me with revulsion. A man with the toothache ought, I know, to have my sympathy, for it is a terrible pain, yet he fills me with nothing but aversion.

I never put off till tomorrow what I can possibly do – the day after.

＊＊＊＊＊＊＊＊＊

Sir Bernard Partridge often told of a dinner party in Tite Street with Oscar and his wife. A chicken was brought in and Oscar took up the carvers and tried to cut a wing but laid them down again wearily, saying:

Constance, why do you give me these ... pedestrians ... to eat?

＊＊＊＊＊＊＊＊＊

To know everything about oneself one must know all about others.

＊＊＊＊＊＊＊＊＊

Wilde dined expensively in Paris, sometimes at the Cafe de Paris. He excused the luxury by saying:

It's a duty we owe to the dignity of letters.

＊＊＊＊＊＊＊＊＊

He once wrote to Sherard: I am hard at work being idle.

Asked by Arthur Balfour what his religion was, he replied:

Well, you know, I don't think I have any. I am an Irish Protestant.

※ ※ ※

To be natural is such a very difficult pose to keep up.

※ ※ ※

It became evident that lectures would not keep the taxgatherer from the door, and one day he was accosted on his Tite Street doorstep. 'I have called about the taxes,' said a little man. Demanded Wilde haughtily:

Taxes! Why should I pay taxes?

'But, sir, you are the householder here, are you not? You live here, you sleep here,' came the reply.

Ah, yes; but then, you see, I sleep so badly.

※ ※ ※

I am the only person in the world I should like to know thoroughly, but I don't see any chance of it just at present.

✿ ✿ ✿

I shall never make a new friend in my life, though perhaps a few after I die.

✿ ✿ ✿

After bringing a friend back to his Merrion Square house he said:

I want to introduce you to my mother. We have founded a Society for the Suppression of Virtue.

✿ ✿ ✿

I was influenced by my mother. Every man is when he is young.

A Woman of No Importance

✿ ✿ ✿

Swinburne is so eloquent that whatever he touches becomes unreal.

✿ ✿ ✿

Mr Henry James writes fiction as if it were a painful duty.

Zola is determined to show that, if he has not got genius, he can at least be dull. And how well he succeeds!

Shakespeare might have met Rozencrantz and Guildenstern in the white streets of London, or seen the serving-men of rival houses bite their thumbs at each other in the open square; but Hamlet came out of his soul, and Romeo out of his passion.

The Critic as Artist

Wordsworth went to the lakes, but he was never a lake poet. He found in stones the sermons he had already hidden there.

The Decay of Lying

Talking of Robert Yelverton Tyrrell, Oscar said:
If he had known less he would have been a poet.

Town life nourishes and perfects all the more civilised elements in man. Shakespeare wrote nothing but doggerel lampoon before he came to London and never penned a line after he left.

One of George Moore's novels, Esther Waters, *drew this comment from him:*
He leads his readers to the latrine and locks them in.

Frank Harris used to boast of his social successes, and of all the grand houses he had stayed at. Oscar, who had reached the limit of boredom, once cut in:
Yes, dear Frank, we believe you – you have dined in every house in London, once.

A lecture by Pater at the London Institution was delivered in a quiet monotonous voice, as if he were reading to himself, and when he enquired of a few friends, 'I hope you all heard me?' Oscar replied for the others:

We overheard you.

❋   ❋   ❋

He told the actor Coquelin that the play he was writing, The Duchess of Padua, *consisted solely of style, and added:*

Between them, Hugo and Shakespeare have exhausted every subject. Originality is no longer possible, even in sin. So there are no real emotions left – only extraordinary adjectives.

❋   ❋   ❋

Whistler, with all his faults, was never guilty of writing a line of poetry.

❋   ❋   ❋

George Moore wrote brilliant English until he discovered grammar.

* * *

Talking of Max Beerbohm, Wilde said:

The Gods bestowed on Max the gift of perpetual old age.

* * *

Bernard Shaw is an excellent man; he has not an enemy in the world, and none of his friends like him.

* * *

Meredith is a prose Browning and so is Browning; he uses poetry as a medium for writing prose.

* * *

Froude was told by Wilde that:

Like most penmen you overrate the power of the sword.

Men and Women

The Book of Life begins with a man and woman in a garden. It ends with Revelations.

A Woman of No Importance

❋　　❋　　❋

Men become old, but they never become good.

Lady Windermere's Fan

❋　　❋　　❋

Mrs Allonby: The Ideal Man ... he should always say much more than he means, and always mean much more than he says.

A Woman of No Importance

A man who can dominate a London dinner-table can dominate the world. The future belongs to the dandy. It is the exquisites who are going to rule.

A Woman of No Importance

There is something tragic about the enormous number of young men there are in England at the present moment who start life with perfect profiles, and end by adopting some useful profession.

Phrases and Philosophies for the Use of the Young

By persistently remaining single, a man converts himself into a permanent public temptation.

Good looks are a snare that every sensible man would like to be caught in.

The Importance of Being Earnest

Men of thought should have nothing to do with action.

Vera, or The Nihilists

The true perfection of man lies, not in what man has, but in what man is.

Man is least himself when he talks in his own person. Give him a mask, and he will tell you the truth.

The Critic as Artist

The mind of a thoroughly well-informed man is a dreadful thing. It is like a bric-a-brac shop, all monsters and dust, with everything priced above its proper value.

The Picture of Dorian Gray

One is tempted to define man as a rational animal who always loses his temper when he is called upon to act in accordance with the dictates of reason.

Intentions

Mrs Allonby: I delight in men over seventy; they always offer one the devotion of a lifetime.

A Woman of No Importance

❊ ❊ ❊

I sometimes think that God, in creating man, somewhat overestimated His ability.

❊ ❊ ❊

No man is rich enough to buy back his past.

An Ideal Husband

❊ ❊ ❊

The evolution of man is slow. The injustice of man is great.

The Soul of Man Under Socialism

❊ ❊ ❊

A man who moralises is usually a hypocrite, and a woman who moralises is invariably plain.

Lady Windermere's Fan

Women – Sphinxes without secrets.

A Woman of No Importance

She is a peacock in everything but beauty.

As long as a woman can look ten years younger than her own daughter, she is perfectly satisfied.

The Picture of Dorian Gray

To be perfectly proportioned is a rare thing in an age when so many women are either over life-size or insignificant.

Lord Arthur Savile's Crime

Women are meant to be loved, not to be understood.

※　　※　　※

Woman begins by resisting a man's advances and ends by blocking his retreat.

※　　※　　※

She wore far too much rouge last night and not quite enough clothes. That is always a sign of despair in a woman.

An Ideal Husband

※　　※　　※

One should never give a woman anything she can't wear in the evening.

An Ideal Husband

※　　※　　※

Miss Prism: A misanthrope I can understand – a woman-thrope, never!

The Importance of Being Earnest

A woman with a past has no future.

If a woman can't make her mistakes charming, she is only a female.

Lord Arthur Savile's Crime

When she is in a very smart gown, she looks like an *edition de luxe* of a wicked French novel meant specially for the English market.

The Importance of Being Earnest

No man has any real success in this world unless he has got women to back him, and women rule society.

She looks like a woman with a past. Most pretty women do.

An Ideal Husband

What have women who have not sinned to do with me, or I with them? We do not understand each other.

A Woman of No Importance

Thirty-five is a very attractive age; London society is full of women of the highest birth who have, of their own free choice, remained thirty-five for years.

The Importance of Being Earnest

Women, as some witty Frenchman once put it, inspire us with the desire to do masterpieces, and always prevent us from carrying them out.

The Picture of Dorian Gray

Women are a decorative sex. They never have anything to say, but they say it charmingly. Women represent the triumph of matter over mind, just as men represent the triumph of mind over morals.

The Picture of Dorian Gray

I don't believe in women thinking too much. Women should think in moderation, as they should do all things in moderation.

A Woman of No Importance

A woman will flirt with anybody in the world as long as other people are looking on.

The Picture of Dorian Gray

The private lives of men and women should not be told to the public. The public have nothing to do with them at all.

The Soul of Man Under Socialism

Modern women understand everything except their husbands.

Between men and women there is no friendship possible. There is passion, enmity, worship, love, but no friendship.

Lady Windermere's Fan

A woman's life revolves in curves of emotion. It is upon lines of intellect that a man's life progresses.

An Ideal Husband

Women are never disarmed by compliments. Men always are. That is the difference between the sexes.

An Ideal Husband

A bad man is the sort of man who admires innocence, and a bad woman is the sort of woman a man never gets tired of.

A Woman of No Importance

It takes a thoroughly good woman to do a thoroughly stupid thing.

Lady Windermere's Fan

I am afraid that women appreciate cruelty, downright cruelty, more than anything else. They have wonderfully primitive instincts. We have emancipated them, but they remain slaves looking for their masters all the same.

The Picture of Dorian Gray

❖ ❖ ❖

Women have a much better time than men in this world; there are far more things forbidden to them.

❖ ❖ ❖

Every woman is a rebel, and usually in wild revolt against herself.

A Woman of No Importance

❖ ❖ ❖

Women are not meant to judge us, but to forgive us when we need forgiveness. Pardon, not punishment, is their mission.

An Ideal Husband

※   ※   ※

No woman should ever be quite accurate about her age – it looks so calculating.

※   ※   ※

The history of women is the history of the worst form of tyranny the world has ever known. The tyranny of the weak over the strong. It is the only tyranny that lasts.

A Woman of No Importance

※   ※   ※

All women become like their mothers. That is their tragedy. No man does. That's his.

The Importance of Being Earnest

※   ※   ※

How hard good women are! How weak bad men are!

Lady Windermere's Fan

Friends and Enemies

I choose my friends for their good looks, my acquaintances for their good characters, and my enemies for their good intellects. A man cannot be too careful in the choice of his enemies.

❊   ❊   ❊

After a good dinner one can forgive anybody, even one's own relations.

A Woman of No Importance

Relations are simply a tedious pack of people, who haven't got the remotest knowledge of how to live, nor the smallest instinct about when to die.

The Importance of Being Earnest

I can't help detesting my relations. I suppose it comes from the fact that none of us stand other people having the same faults as ourselves.

The Picture of Dorian Gray

No one cares about distant relations nowadays. They went out of fashion years ago.

Lord Arthur Savile's Crime

I dare say that if I knew him I should not be his friend at all. It is a very dangerous thing to know one's friends.

The Remarkable Rocket

I think that generosity is the essence of friendship.

The Devoted Friend

I always like to know everything about my new friends, and nothing about my old ones.

The Picture of Dorian Gray

One has a right to judge a man by the effect he has over his friends.

The Picture of Dorian Gray

What is the good of friendship if one cannot say exactly what one means?

The Devoted Friend

An acquaintance that begins with a compliment is sure to develop into a real friendship. It starts in the right manner.

An Ideal Husband

Laughter is not at all a bad beginning for a friendship, and it is far the best ending for one.

The Picture of Dorian Gray

Young and Old

The secret of remaining young is never to have an emotion that is unbecoming.

The Picture of Dorian Gray

An inordinate passion for pleasure is the secret of remaining young.

Lord Arthur Savile's Crime

Youth isn't an affectation. Youth is an art.

An Ideal Husband

The pulse of joy that beats in us at twenty becomes sluggish. Our limbs fail, our senses rot. We degenerate into hideous puppets, haunted by the memory of the passions of which we were too much afraid, and the exquisite temptations that we had not the courage to yield to. Youth! Youth! There is absolutely nothing in the world but youth!

The Picture of Dorian Gray

The tragedy of old age is not that one is old, but that one is young.

The Picture of Dorian Gray

The condition of perfection is idleness; the aim of perfection is youth.

Phrases and Philosophies for the Use of the Young

Fathers should be neither seen nor heard; that is the only proper basis for family life.

※　　※　　※

To get back one's youth, one has merely to repeat one's follies.

The Picture of Dorian Gray

※　　※　　※

The old believe everything; the middle-aged suspect everything; the young know everything.

Phrases and Philosophies for the Use of the Young

※　　※　　※

Few parents nowadays pay any regard to what children say to them. The old-fashioned respect for the young is fast dying.

The Importance of Being Earnest

※　　※　　※

To lose one parent ... may be regarded as a misfortune; to lose both looks like carelessness.

The Importance of Being Earnest

❋ ❋ ❋

Children begin by loving their parents. After a time they judge them. Rarely, if ever, do they forgive them.

A Woman of No Importance

❋ ❋ ❋

The soul is born old but grows young. That is the comedy of life. And the body is born young and grows old. That is life's tragedy.

A Woman of No Importance

❋ ❋ ❋

Youth is the one thing worth having.

The Picture of Dorian Gray

❋ ❋ ❋

The best way to make children is to make them happy.

Rags and
Riches

I t is better to have a permanent income
than to be fascinating.

The Model Millionaire

Gold-tipped cigarettes are awfully expensive. I can only afford them when I am in debt.

A Woman of No Importance

It is very vulgar to talk about one's business. Only people like stockbrokers do that, and then merely at dinner parties.

The Importance of Being Earnest

He rides in the Row at ten o'clock in the morning, goes to the Opera three times a week, changes his clothes at least five times a day, and dines out every night of the season. You don't call that leading an idle life, do you?

An Ideal Husband

Young people, nowadays, imagine that money is everything, and when they grow older they know it.

The Picture of Dorian Gray

I don't want money. It is people who pay their bills who want that, and I never pay mine.

The Picture of Dorian Gray

Ordinary riches can be stolen from a man. Real riches cannot. In the treasure-house of your soul, there are infinitely precious things that may not be taken from you.

The Soul of Man Under Socialism

There are many things that we would throw away, if we were not afraid that others might pick them up.

The Picture of Dorian Gray

It is only by not paying one's bills that one can hope to live in the memory of the commercial classes.

Phrases and Philosophies for the Use of the Young

As for begging it is safer to beg than to take, but it is finer to take than to beg.

The Soul of Man Under Socialism

Nowadays we are all of us so hard up that the only pleasant things to pay are compliments. They're the only things we can pay.

Lady Windermere's Fan

I should fancy that the real tragedy of the poor is that they can afford nothing but self-denial.

The Picture of Dorian Gray

There is only one class in the community that thinks more about money than the rich, and that is the poor. The poor can think of nothing else.

The Soul of Man Under Socialism

What between the duties expected of one during one's lifetime, and the duties exacted from one after one's death, land has ceased to be either a profit or a pleasure.

The Importance of Being Earnest

Credit is the capital of a younger son.

The Picture of Dorian Gray

Saints and Sinners

The only difference between the saint and sinner is that every saint has a past, and every sinner has a future.

A Woman of No Importance

❁   ❁   ❁

There are terrible temptations that it required strength, strength and courage, to yield to.

An Ideal Husband

Every impulse that we strive to strangle broods in the mind and poisons us. ... The only way to get rid of temptation is to yield to it.

I can resist everything except temptation.
Lady Windermere's Fan

The sick do not ask if the hand that smoothes their pillow is pure, nor the dying care if the lips that touch their brow have known the kiss of sin.
A Woman of No Importance

He hasn't a single redeeming vice.

I hope you have not been leading a double life, pretending to be wicked and being really good all the time. That would be hypocrisy.

The Importance of Being Earnest

Sin is a thing that writes itself across a man's face. It cannot be concealed.

The Picture of Dorian Gray

Starvation, and not sin, is the parent of modern crime.

The Soul of Man Under Socialism

Nothing makes one so vain as being told that one is a sinner.

The Picture of Dorian Gray

Everything you have said today seems to me excessively immoral. It has been interesting listening to you.

A Woman of No Importance

I love scandals about other people, but scandals about myself don't interest me. They have not got the charm of novelty.

The Picture of Dorian Gray

Murder is always a mistake ... One should never do anything that one cannot talk about after dinner.

The Picture of Dorian Gray

What a Communist he is! He would have an equal distribution of sin as well as property.

Vera, or The Nihilists

Agitators are a set of interfering, meddling people, who come down to some perfectly contented class of the community and sow the seeds of discontent amongst them. That is the reason why agitators are so absolutely necessary.

The Soul of Man Under Socialism

One should never make one's debut with a scandal. One should reserve that to give an interest to one's old age.

The Picture of Dorian Gray

He would stab his best friend for the sake of writing an epigram on his tombstone.

Vera, or The Nihilists

When we are happy we are always good, but when we are good we are not always happy.

The Picture of Dorian Gray

The one advantage of playing with fire is that one never gets even singed. It is the people who don't know how to play with it who get burned up.

A Woman of No Importance

Conscience and cowardice are really the same things. Conscience is the trade-name of the firm.

The Picture of Dorian Gray

If we lived long enough to see the results of our actions it may be that those who call themselves good would be sickened with a dull remorse, and those whom the world calls evil stirred by a noble joy.

The Critic as Artist

❈   ❈   ❈

Humanity takes itself too seriously. It is the world's original sin. If the cavemen had known how to laugh, history would have been different.

❈   ❈   ❈

Good taste is the excuse I've always given for leading such a bad life.

The Importance of Being Earnest

❈   ❈   ❈

I like men who have a future and women who have a past.

The Picture of Dorian Gray

❈   ❈   ❈

I prefer women with a past. They're always so damned amusing to talk to.

Lady Windermere's Fan

❈   ❈   ❈

Wicked women bother one. Good women bore one. That is the only difference between them.

Lady Windermere's Fan

I don't think now that people can be divided into the good and the bad as though they were two separate races or creatures. What are called good women may have terrible things in them, mad moods of recklessness, assertion, jealousy, sin. Bad women, as they are termed, may have in them sorrow, repentance, pity, sacrifice.

Lady Windermere's Fan

Immoral women are rarely attractive. What made her quite irresistible was that she was unmoral.

If a woman really repents, she never wishes to return to the society that has made or seen her ruin.

Lady Windermere's Fan

When a man is old enough to do wrong he should be old enough to do right also.

A Woman of No Importance

He has one of those terribly weak natures that are not susceptible to influence.

An Ideal Husband

A man cannot always be estimated by what he does. He may keep the law, and yet be worthless. He may break the law and yet be fine.

The Soul of Man Under Socialism

How many men are there in modern life who would like to see their past burning to white ashes before them?

An Ideal Husband

It is a dangerous thing to reform anyone.

Lady Windermere's Fan

No crime is vulgar, but all vulgarity is crime. Vulgarity is the conduct of others.

Phrases and Philosophies for the Use of the Young

I dislike arguments of any kind. They are always vulgar, and often convincing.

The Importance of Being Earnest

I can stand brute force, but brute reason is quite unbearable. There is something unfair about its use. It is hitting below the intellect.

❋ ❋ ❋

It is only the intellectually lost who ever argue.

❋ ❋ ❋

The only horrible thing in the world is *ennui*. That is the one sin for which there is no forgiveness.

❋ ❋ ❋

We are not sent into the world to air our moral prejudices.

❋ ❋ ❋

What people call insincerity is simply a method by which we can multiply our personalities.

Nothing looks so like innocence as an indiscretion.

Lord Arthur Savile's Crime

Surely Providence can resist temptation by this time.

Lord Arthur Savile's Crime

It is better to be beautiful than to be good, but it is better to be good than to be ugly.

Society often forgives the criminal; it never forgives the dreamer.

The Critic as Artist

As one reads history ... one is absolutely sickened, not by the crimes that the wicked have committed, but by the punishments that the good have inflicted; and a community is infinitely more brutalised by the habitual employment of punishment than it is by the occasional occurrences of crime.

After all, what is a fine lie? Simply that which is its own evidence.

The Decay of Lying

As for believing things, I can believe anything, provided that it is quite incredible.

The Picture of Dorian Gray

People have a careless way of talking about a 'born liar', just as they talk about a born poet. Lying and poetry are arts – arts, as Plato saw, not unconnected with each other – and they require the most careful study, the most interested devotion.

The Decay of Lying

If one tells the truth, one is sure, sooner or later, to be found out.

Phrases and Philosophies for the Use of the Young

It is a terrible thing for a man to find out suddenly that all his life he has been speaking nothing but the truth.

The Importance of Being Earnest

Modern morality consists in accepting the standard of one's age. I consider that for any man of culture to accept the standard of his age is a form of the grossest immorality.

The Picture of Dorian Gray

Good resolutions are useless attempts to interfere with scientific laws. Their origin is pure vanity. Their result is absolutely nil. They give us, now and then, some of those luxurious sterile emotions that have a certain charm for the weak. That is all that can be said of them. They are simply cheques that men draw on a bank where they have no account.

The Picture of Dorian Gray

If you pretend to be good, the world takes you very seriously. If you pretend to be bad, it doesn't. Such is the astounding stupidity of optimism.

Lady Windermere's Fan

⁂

You will soon be going about like the con-
verted and the revivalist, warning people against
all the sins of which you have grown tired.

The Picture of Dorian Gray

⁂

As a wicked man I am a complete failure. Why,
there are lots of people who say I have never
really done anything wrong in the whole course
of my life. Of course, they only say it behind my
back.

Lady Windermere's Fan

⁂

Crime in England is rarely the result of sin. It
is nearly always the result of starvation.

Pen, Pencil and Poison

⁂

There is no sin except stupidity.

The Critic as Artist

＊ ＊ ＊

The basis of every scandal is an immoral certainty.

The Picture of Dorian Gray

＊ ＊ ＊

Society sooner or later must return to its lost leader, the cultured and fascinating liar.

The Decay of Lying

Love and Marriage

Marriage is hardly a thing that one can do now and then – except in America.

The Picture of Dorian Gray

❖   ❖   ❖

Women have been so highly educated that nothing should surprise them except happy marriages.

❖   ❖   ❖

Twenty years of romance make a woman look like a ruin; but twenty years of marriage make her look like a public building.

A Woman of No Importance

❋ ❋ ❋

How marriage ruins a man! It's as demoralising as cigarettes, and far more expensive.

Lady Windermere's Fan

❋ ❋ ❋

A man who desires to get married should know either everything or nothing.

❋ ❋ ❋

The proper basis for marriage is a mutual misunderstanding.

Lord Arthur Savile's Crime

❋ ❋ ❋

Marriage is the one subject on which all women agree and all men disagree.

❈   ❈   ❈

Mrs Cheveley: Their husbands. That is the one thing the modern woman never understands.

Lady Markby: And a very good thing too, dear, I dare say. It might break up many a happy home if they did.

An Ideal Husband

❈   ❈   ❈

Nowadays all the married men are like bachelors, and all the bachelors like married men.

The Picture of Dorian Gray

❈   ❈   ❈

All men are married women's property. That is the only true definition of what married women's property really is.

A Woman of No Importance

❈   ❈   ❈

One can always recognise women who trust their husbands; they look so thoroughly unhappy.

❖　　❖　　❖

Her capacity for family affection is extraordinary. When her third husband died, her hair turned quite gold from grief.

The Picture of Dorian Gray

❖　　❖　　❖

When a woman marries again, it is because she detested her first husband. When a man marries again, it is because he adored his first wife. Women try their luck; men risk theirs.

The Picture of Dorian Gray

❖　　❖　　❖

It is a curious thing about the game of marriage – the wives hold all the honours, and invariably lose the odd trick.

Lady Windermere's Fan

The husbands of very beautiful women belong to the criminal classes.

The Picture of Dorian Gray

Where there is no exaggeration there is no love, and where there is no love there is no understanding.

For an artist to marry his model is as fatal as for a gourmet to marry his cook; the one gets no sittings, and the other no dinners.

He once said of a famous actress who, after a tragic domestic life, had married a fool:

She thought that, because he was stupid, he would be kindly, when, of course, kindliness requires imagination and intellect.

Men are horribly tedious when they are good husbands, and abominably conceited when they are not.

A Woman of No Importance

No man should have a secret from his wife – she invariably finds it out.

There's nothing in the world like the devotion of a married woman. It's a thing no married man knows anything about.

Lady Windermere's Fan

When a man has once loved a woman, he will do anything for her, except continue to love her.

Lady Windermere: I don't like compliments, and I don't see why a man should think he is pleasing a woman enormously when he says to her a whole heap of things that he doesn't mean.

Lady Windermere's Fan

More women grow old nowadays through the faithfulness of their admirers than through anything else.

Women are meant to be loved, not to be understood.

The Sphinx Without a Secret

❖ ❖ ❖

I don't think there is a woman in the world who would not be a little flattered if one made love to her. It is that which makes women so irresistibly adorable.

A Woman of No Importance

❖ ❖ ❖

She'll never love you unless you are always at her heels; women like to be bothered.

Vera, or The Nihilists

❖ ❖ ❖

Plain women are always jealous of their husbands. Beautiful women never have time. They are always so occupied in being jealous of other people's husbands.

A Woman of No Importance

It is perfectly brutal the way most women nowadays behave to men who are not their husbands.

Lady Windermere's Fan

I don't mind plain women being Puritans. It is the only excuse they have for being plain.

A Woman of No Importance

Women give to men the very gold of their lives. But they invariably want it back in small change.

I am sick of women who love me. Women who hate me are much more interesting.

The Picture of Dorian Gray

The only way to behave to a woman is to make love to her, if she is pretty, and to someone else, if she is plain

The Importance of Being Earnest

In the case of very fascinating women, sex is a challenge, not a defence.

An Ideal Husband

There is only one real tragedy in a woman's life. The fact that her past is always her lover, and her future invariably her husband.

An Ideal Husband

As a rule, people who act lead the most commonplace lives. They are good husbands or faithful wives, or something tedious.

The Picture of Dorian Gray

People are either hunting for husbands or hiding from them.

An Ideal Husband

Men marry because they are tired; women because they are curious; both are disappointed.

The Picture of Dorian Gray

The one charm of marriage is that it makes a life of deception absolutely necessary for both parties.

The Picture of Dorian Gray

I have often observed that in married households the champagne is rarely of a first-rate brand.

The Importance of Being Earnest

The amount of women in London who flirt with their own husbands is perfectly scandalous. It looks so bad. It is simply washing one's clean linen in public.

The Importance of Being Earnest

The happiness of a married man depends on the people he has not married.

A Woman of No Importance

The happiness of a married man depends on the people he has not married.

A Woman of No Importance

If we men married the women we deserve we should have a very bad time of it.

An Ideal Husband

Mrs Allonby: My husband is a sort of promissory note; I'm tired of meeting him.

A Woman of No Importance

There is nothing so difficult to marry as a large nose.

An Ideal Husband

❈   ❈   ❈

Love is an illusion.

The Picture of Dorian Gray

❈   ❈   ❈

Nothing spoils a romance so much as a sense of humour in the woman – or the want of it in the man.

A Woman of No Importance

❈   ❈   ❈

They do not sin at all /
Who sin for love.

The Duchess of Padua

❈   ❈   ❈

One should always be in love. That is the reason one should never marry.

❋   ❋   ❋

Men always want to be a woman's first love. That is their clumsy vanity. Women have a more subtle instinct about things; what they like is to be a man's last romance.

A Woman of No Importance

❋   ❋   ❋

Romance is the privilege of the rich, not the profession of the poor.

The Model Millionaire

❋   ❋   ❋

The very essence of romance is uncertainty. If ever I get married, I'll certainly try to forget the fact.

The Importance of Being Earnest

❋   ❋   ❋

Once a week is quite enough to propose to anyone, and it should always be done in a manner that attracts some attention.

An Ideal Husband

✦ ✦ ✦

It is not the perfect but the imperfect who have need of love.

An Ideal Husband

✦ ✦ ✦

I am not at all romantic. I am not old enough. I leave romance to my seniors.

An Ideal Husband

✦ ✦ ✦

A kiss may ruin a human life.

A Woman of No Importance

✦ ✦ ✦

If one really loves a woman, all other women in the world become absolutely meaningless to one.

Lady Windermere's Fan

❖   ❖   ❖

Who, being loved, is poor?

A Woman of No Importance

❖   ❖   ❖

A man can be happy with any woman as long as he does not love her.

The Picture of Dorian Gray

❖   ❖   ❖

Those who are faithful know only the trivial side of love: it is the faithless who know love's tragedies.

The Picture of Dorian Gray

❖   ❖   ❖

Young men want to be faithful and are not; old men want to be faithless and cannot.

The Picture of Dorian Gray

❈　　❈　　❈

The only difference between a caprice and a lifelong passion is that the caprice lasts a little longer.

The Picture of Dorian Gray

❈　　❈　　❈

Polygamy – how much more poetic it is to marry one and love many.

❈　　❈　　❈

Divorces are made in heaven.

People and
Public

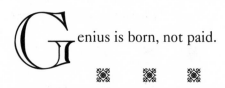enius is born, not paid.

I am very fond of the public, and personally I always patronise the public very much.

You can't go anywhere without meeting clever people. The thing has become an absolute public nuisance. I wish to goodness we had a few fools left.

The Importance of Being Earnest

I like persons better than principles and I like persons with no principles better than anything else in the world.

The Picture of Dorian Gray

❈   ❈   ❈

The clever people never listen, and the stupid people never talk.

A Woman of No Importance

❈   ❈   ❈

Only dull people are brilliant at breakfast.

An Ideal Husband

❈   ❈   ❈

Whenever people talk to me about the weather, I always feel certain that they mean something else.

The Importance of Being Earnest

❈   ❈   ❈

Nowadays people know the price of everything and the value of nothing.

The Picture of Dorian Gray

It is only the shallow people who do not judge by appearances.

The Picture of Dorian Gray

Most people are other people. Their thoughts are someone else's opinions, their lives a mimicry, their passions a quotation.

The public have an insatiable curiosity to know everything, except what is worth knowing.

The Soul of Man Under Socialism

The public is wonderfully tolerant. It forgives everything except genius.

The Critic as Artist

One can always be kind to people about whom one cares nothing.

The Picture of Dorian Gray

It is absurd to divide people into good and bad. People are either charming or tedious.

Lady Windermere's Fan

There are only two kinds of people who are really fascinating – people who know absolutely everything and people who know absolutely nothing.

The Picture of Dorian Gray

I'm sure I don't know half the people who come to my house. Indeed, from all I hear, I shouldn't like to.

An Ideal Husband

It is perfectly monstrous the way people go about nowadays saying things against one behind one's back that are absolutely and entirely true.

The Picture of Dorian Gray

England and the English

The English have a miraculous power of turning wine into water.

The English young lady is the dragon of good taste.

An Ideal Husband

But there is no literary public in England for anything except newspapers, primers and encyclopaedias. Of all the people in the world the English have the least sense of the beauty of literature.

The Picture of Dorian Gray

No modern literary work of any worth has been produced in English by an English writer – except of course Bradshaw.

Englishwomen conceal their feelings till after they are married. They show them then.

A Woman of No Importance

England will never be civilised until she has added Utopia to her dominions.

The Critic as Artist

I don't desire to change anything in England except the weather.

The Picture of Dorian Gray

Mrs Cheveley: A typical Englishman, always dull and usually violent.

An Ideal Husband

The *Peerage* is the one book a young man about town should know thoroughly and it is the best thing in fiction the English have ever done.

A Woman of No Importance

The real weakness of England lies, not in incomplete armaments or unfortified coasts, not in the poverty that creeps through sunless lanes, or the drunkenness that brawls in loathsome courts, but simply in the fact that her ideals are emotional and not intellectual.

The Critic as Artist

In this country it is enough for a man to have distinction and brains for every common tongue to wag against him. And what sort of lives do these people who pose as being moral lead themselves? We are in the native land of the hypocrite.

The Picture of Dorian Gray

In England, at any rate, education produces no effect whatsoever. If it did, it would prove a serious danger to the upper classes, and would probably lead to acts of violence in Grosvenor Square.

The Importance of Being Earnest

Flowers are as common in the country as people are in London.

Extraordinary thing about the lower classes in England – they are always losing their relations. They are extremely fortunate in that respect.

An Ideal Husband

Lord Caversham: Can't make out how you stand London society. The thing has gone to the dogs, a lot of damned nobodies talking about nothing.

An Ideal Husband

If one could only teach the English how to talk, and the Irish how to listen, society here would be quite civilised.

An Ideal Husband

I love London society! I think it has immensely improved. It is entirely composed now of beautiful idiots and brilliant lunatics. Just what society should be.

An Ideal Husband

To be pretty is the best fashion there is, and the only fashion that England succeeds in setting.

An Ideal Husband

The British cook is a foolish woman who should be turned for her iniquities into a pillar of salt which she never knows how to use.

London thoroughfares:
Wearied of the houses you turn to contemplate the street itself, you have nothing to look at but chimney-pot hats, men with sandwich boards, vermilion letter-boxes, and do that even at the risk of being run over by an emerald-green omnibus.

In England a man who can't talk morality twice a week to a large, popular, immoral audience is quite over as a serious politician. There would be nothing left for him as a profession except Botany or the Church.

An Ideal Husband

Sound English common sense – the inherited stupidity of the race.

I live in the East End because there the people don't wear masks, explained Olive Schreiner. Explained Oscar Wilde:

And I live in the West End because there they do.

To disagree with three-fourths of the British public on all points is one of the first elements of sanity, one of the deepest consolations in all moments of spiritual doubt.

If in the last century she [England] tried to govern Ireland with an insolence that was intensified by race hatred and religious prejudice, she has sought to rule her in this century with a stupidity that is aggravated by good intentions.

I need hardly say that we were delighted and amused at the typical English way in which our ideas were misunderstood. They took our epigrams as earnest, and our parodies as prose.

The English have really everything in common with the Americans, except, of course, language.

※　　　※　　　※

One knows so well the popular idea of health. The English country gentleman galloping after a fox – the unspeakable in full pursuit of the uneatable.

A Woman of No Importance

※　　　※　　　※

Thinking is the most unhealthy thing in the world, and people die of it just as they die of any other disease. Fortunately, in England at any rate, thought is not catching. Our splendid physique as a people is entirely due to our national stupidity.

The Decay of Lying

※　　　※　　　※

On the British race:

It represents the survival of the pushing.

The Picture of Dorian Gray

※　　※　　※

The English can't stand a man who is always saying he is right, but they are very fond of a man who admits he has been in the wrong.

An Ideal Husband

※　　※　　※

There are only five women in London worth talking to and two of these can't be admitted into decent society.

※　　※　　※

English actors act quite well but they act best between the lines.

America and
the Americans

Of course America had often been discovered before Columbus, but it had always been hushed up.

❋　　❋　　❋

Perhaps, after all, America never has been discovered. I myself would say that it had merely been detected.

The Picture of Dorian Gray

❋　　❋　　❋

The youth of America is their oldest tradition. It has been going on now for three hundred years. To hear them talk we would imagine they were in their first childhood. As far as civilisation goes they are in their second.

※ ※ ※

Six aspects of American life caught his immediate attention:

(1) Everybody seems in a hurry to catch a train. This is a state of things which is not favourable to poetry or romance.

(2) It is the noisiest country that ever existed. Such continual turmoil must ultimately be destructive of the musical faculty.

(3) There are no trappings, no pageants, and no gorgeous ceremonies. I saw only two processions: one was the Fire Brigade preceded by the Police; the other was the Police preceded by the Fire Brigade.

(4) In America life is one long expectoration.

(5) Why does not science, instead of troubling itself about sunspots, which nobody ever saw, or,

if they did, ought not to speak about, why does not science busy itself with drainage and sanitary engineering? Why does it not clean the streets and free the rivers from pollution?

(6) I believe a most serious problem for the American people to consider is the cultivation of better manners. It is the most noticeable, the most painful, defect in American civilisation.

American girls are as clever at concealing their parents as English women are at concealing their past.

The Picture of Dorian Gray

On American girls:

Pretty and charming – little oases of pretty unreasonableness in a vast desert of practical common sense.

All Americans lecture ... I suppose it is something in their climate.

A Woman of No Importance

Niagara Falls he described as:

Simply a vast unnecessary amount of water going the wrong way and then falling over unnecessary rocks.

The Mississippi was in flood, yellow, raging, hissing, rushing, and he remarked that:

No well-behaved river ought to act that way.

To a newspaperman at Cincinnati he said:

I wonder your criminals don't plead the ugliness of your city as an excuse for their crimes.

❋   ❋   ❋

In San Francisco he told his listeners that pictures ought to be hung on the eye-line:

The habit in America of hanging them up near the cornice struck me as irrational at first. It was not until I saw how bad the pictures were that I realised the advantage of the custom.

❋   ❋   ❋

In the Rockies I saw the only rational method of art criticism I have ever come across. Over the piano was printed a notice: 'Please do not shoot the pianist: he is doing his best.' The mortality among pianists in that place is marvellous.

❋   ❋   ❋

On being told that Rossetti, in order to get rid of a poet who was always cadging, had given him enough money to go to the States, Wilde drawled:

Of course, if one had the money to go to America, one would not go.

❊ ❊ ❊

For the American, he felt:
Art has no marvel, and Beauty no meaning, and the Past no message.

❊ ❊ ❊

America reminds me of one of Edgar Allan Poe's exquisite poems, because it is full of belles.

❊ ❊ ❊

I would rather have discovered Mrs Lily Langtry than have discovered America.

❊ ❊ ❊

The Americans are certainly great hero-worshippers, and always take their heroes from the criminal classes.

American women are charming, but American men – alas!

Some Southern Americans have a melancholy tendency to date every event of importance by the late war. 'How beautiful the moon is tonight,' I once remarked to a gentleman standing near me. 'Yes,' was his reply, 'but you should have seen it before the war.'

After receiving a wire from Griggsville asking him to 'lecture us on aesthetics', he replied:

Begin by changing the name of your town.

I opened a new vein, or lode, with a silver drill, the lode being named 'The Oscar'. I had hoped that in their grand simple way they would have offered me shares in 'The Oscar', but in their artless untutored fashion they did not.

While in Denver he was told that if he went ahead with his plans to visit Leadville the tougher spirits would be sure to shoot him or his travelling manager.

I wrote and told them that nothing that they could do to my travelling manager would intimidate me.

When I was at Leadville and reflected that all the shining silver that I saw coming from the mines would be made into ugly dollars, it made me sad.

American reporters wanted to know why he carried his fur coat about with him. His reply:

To hide the hideous sofas in all the hotel rooms.

So infinitesimal did I find the knowledge of Art, west of the Rocky Mountains, that an art patron – one who in his day had been a miner – actually sued the railroad company for damages because the plaster-cast Venus de Milo, which he had imported from Paris, had been delivered minus the arms. And, what is more surprising still, he gained his case and the damages.

While playing poker he suggested it was:

Like most of the distinctly national products of America, and seems to have been imported from abroad.

It is only fair to admit that he [the American] can exaggerate; but even his exaggeration has a rational basis. It is not founded on wit or fancy; it does not spring from any poetic imagination; it is simply an earnest attempt on the part of the language to keep pace with the enormous size of the country. It is evident that where it takes one twenty-four hours to go across a single parish, and seven days' steady railway travelling to keep a dinner engagement in another State, the ordinary resources of human speech are quite inadequate to the strain put on them, and new linguistic forms have to be invented, new methods of description resorted to. But this is nothing more than the fatal influence of geography upon adjectives; for naturally humorous the American man certainly is not.

'They say that when good Americans die they go to Paris,' chuckled Sir Thomas ...

'Really! And where do bad Americans go to when they die?' inquired the Duchess.

'They go to America,' murmured Lord Henry.
The Picture of Dorian Gray

❖   ❖   ❖

The crude commercialism of America, its materialist spirit, its indifference to the poetical side of things, and its lack of imagination and of high unattainable ideals, are entirely due to that country having adopted for its national hero a man who, according to his own confession, was incapable of telling a lie, and it is not too much to say that the story of George Washington and the cherry-tree has done more harm, and in a shorter space of time, than any other moral tale in the whole of literature – and the amusing part of the whole thing is that the story of the cherry-tree is an absolute myth.

The Decay of Lying

... And Some Others

The great superiority of France over England is that in France every bourgeois wants to be an artist, whereas in England every artist wants to be a bourgeois.

In Paris one can lose one's time most delightfully; but one can never lose one's way.

Nothing is impossible in Russia but reform.

Vera, or The Nihilists

A Russian who lives happily under the present system of government in Russia must either believe that man has no soul, or that, if he has, it is not worth developing.

The Soul of Man Under Socialism

Greek dress was in its essence inartistic. Nothing should reveal the body but the body.

Phrases and Philosophies for the Use of the Young

When I look at the map and see what an ugly country Australia is, I feel that I want to go there and see if it cannot be changed into a more beautiful form!

He described Jewish money-lenders as:
Gentlemen who breathe through their noses and make you pay through yours.

But he nevertheless thought that hostility to Jews was:
Vulgar and ungrateful: they are the only people who lend money.

For a man to be both a genius and a Scotsman is the very stage for tragedy. ... Your Scotsman believes only in success. ... God saved the genius of Robert Burns to poetry by driving him through drink to failure.

To fail and to die young is the only hope for a Scotsman who wishes to remain an artist.

Art and Artists

rtists, like Gods, must never leave their pedestals.

The past is of no importance. The present is of no importance. It is with the future that we have to deal. For the past is what man should not have been. The present is what man ought not to be. The future is what artists are.

The Soul of Man Under Socialism

The only artists I have ever known who are personally delightful are bad artists. Good artists exist simply in what they make and consequently are perfectly uninteresting in what they are.

The Picture of Dorian Gray

No work of art ever puts forward views. Views belong to people who are not artists.

Journalists record only what happens. What does it matter what happens? It is only the abiding things that are interesting, not the horrid incidents of everyday life. Creation for the joy of creation is the aim of the artist, and that is why the artist is a more divine type than the saint.

I am always amused by the silly vanity of those writers and artists of our day who seem to imagine that the primary function of the critic is to chatter about their second-rate work.

The Critic as Artist

※　　　※　　　※

People sometimes enquire what form of government it is most suitable for an artist to live under. To this question there is only one answer. The form of government that is most suitable to the artist is no government at all.

The Soul of Man Under Socialism

※　　　※　　　※

At present the newspapers are trying hard to induce the public to judge a sculptor, for instance, never by his statues but by the way he treats his wife; a painter by the amount of his income; and a poet by the colour of his necktie.

※　　　※　　　※

When the public say a work is grossly

unintelligible, they mean that the artist has said or made a beautiful thing that is new. When they describe a work as grossly immoral, they mean that the artist has said or made a beautiful thing that is true.

The Soul of Man Under Socialism

There is hardly a single person in the House of Commons worth painting, though many of them would be the better for a little whitewashing.

The only portraits in which one believes are portraits where there is very little of the sitter and a very great deal of the artist.

The Decay of Lying

Most of our modern portrait painters are doomed to oblivion. They never paint what they see. They paint what the public sees, and the public never sees anything.

The Decay of Living

No great artist ever sees things as they really are. If he did he would cease to be an artist.

The Decay of Lying

She is like most artists; she is all style without any sincerity.

The Nightingale and the Rose

It is only an auctioneer who can equally and impartially admire all schools of art.

The Critic as Artist

Nobody of any real culture ever talks about the beauty of a sunset. Sunsets are quite old-fashioned. They belong to the time when Turner was the last note in art. To admire them is a distinct sign of provincialism. Upon the other hand they go on. Yesterday evening Mrs Arundel insisted on my going to the window and looking at the glorious sky, as she called it. Of course I had to look at it. She is one of those absurdly pretty Philistines to whom one can deny nothing. And what was it? It was simply a very second-rate Turner, a Turner of bad period, with all the painter's worst faults exaggerated and over-emphasised.

The Decay of Lying

One should either be a work of art, or wear a work of art.

Phrases and Philosophies for the Use of the Young

A really well-made buttonhole is the only link between Art and Nature.

Phrases and Philosophies for the Use of the Young

※　　　※　　　※

The telling of beautiful untrue things is the proper aim of art.

The Decay of Lying

※　　　※　　　※

All art is at once surface and symbol. Those who go beneath the surface do so at their peril. Those who read the symbol do so at their peril.

The Picture of Dorian Gray

※　　　※　　　※

To reveal art and conceal the artist is art's aim.

The Picture of Dorian Gray

※　　　※　　　※

The proper school to learn art is not Life but Art.

The Decay of Lying

We can forgive a man for making a useful thing as long as he does not admire it. The only excuse for making a useless thing is that one admires it intensely. All art is quite useless.

The Picture of Dorian Gray

Art is the most intense mode of individualism that the world has known.

The Soul of Man Under Socialism

The best that one can say of most modern creative art is that it is just a little less vulgar than reality.

The Critic as Artist

All art is immoral. For emotion for the sake of emotion is the aim of art, and emotion for the sake of action is the aim of life.

The Critic as Artist

Nature is elbowing her way into the charmed circle of Art.

Nature is always behind the age. It takes a great artist to be thoroughly modern.

On seeing the painter Frith's Derby Day, *which was bought for the nation, he reverently asked:*

Is it really all done by hand?

That curious mixture of bad painting and good intentions that always entitles a man to be called a representative British artist.

It is the spectator, and not life, that art really mirrors.

The Picture of Dorian Gray

Modern pictures are, no doubt, delightful to look at. At least, some of them are. But they are quite impossible to live with; they are too clever, too assertive, too intellectual. Their meaning is too obvious, and their method too clearly defined. One exhausts what they have to say in a very short time, and then they become as tedious as one's relations.

The Critic as Artist

❈　　❈　　❈

Art is rarely intelligible to the criminal classes.

❈　　❈　　❈

The first duty of an art critic is to hold his tongue at all times, and upon all subjects.

The English Renaissance of Art

Writers and Writing

I never write plays for anyone. I write plays to amuse myself. After, if people want to act in them, I sometimes allow them to do so.

※ ※ ※

Talking of the small number of his poems In Memoriam *that had been published:*

My first idea was to print only three copies; one for myself, one for the British Museum, and one for Heaven. I had some doubt about the British Museum.

※ ※ ※

Wilde's admiration for the academic evaporated soon after university and he said that statements in a book on Italian Literature showed:

A want of knowledge that must be the result of years of study.

※　　※　　※

I hate vulgar realism in literature. The man who could call a spade a spade should be compelled to use one. It is the only thing he is fit for.

The Picture of Dorian Gray

※　　※　　※

The ancient historians gave us delightful fiction in the form of fact; the modern novelist presents us with dull facts under the guise of fiction.

The Decay of Lying

※　　※　　※

I was working on the proof of one of my poems all the morning, and took out a comma. In the afternoon I put it back again.

❋ ❋ ❋

At twilight nature becomes a wonderfully suggestive effect, and is not without loveliness, though perhaps its chief use is to illustrate quotations from the poets.

The Decay of Lying

❋ ❋ ❋

The truth is rarely pure and never simple. Modern life would be very tedious if it were either, and modern literature a complete impossibility.

The Importance of Being Earnest

❋ ❋ ❋

Journalism is unreadable, and literature is not read.

The Critic as Artist

All bad poetry springs from genuine feeling. To be natural is to be obvious, and to be obvious is to be inartistic.

The Critic as Artist

Any place you love is the world to you ... but love is not fashionable any more: the poets have killed it. They wrote so much about it that nobody believed them, and I am not surprised.

The Remarkable Rocket

About his own play The Importance of Being Earnest *he said:*

The first act is ingenious, the second beautiful, the third abominably clever.

Literature always anticipates life. It does not copy it, but moulds it to its purpose. The nineteenth century, as we know it, is largely an invention of Balzac.

The Decay of Lying

A poet can survive anything but a misprint.

Anybody can write a three-volumed novel. It merely requires a complete ignorance of both life and literature.

The Critic as Artist

The books that the world calls immoral books are books that show the world its own shame.

The Picture of Dorian Gray

We have been able to have fine poetry in England because the public do not read it, and consequently do not influence it.

The Soul of Man Under Socialism

I quite admit that modern novels have many good points. All I insist on is that, as a class, they are quite unreadable.

The Decay of Lying

A great poet, a really great poet, is the most unpoetical of creatures. But inferior poets are absolutely fascinating. The worse their rhymes the more picturesque they look. The mere fact of having published a book of second-rate sonnets makes a man quite irresistible. He lives the poetry he cannot write. The others write the poetry that they dare not realise.

The Picture of Dorian Gray

I never travel without my diary. One should always have something sensational to read in the train.

The Importance of Being Earnest

The only real people are the people who never existed and if a novelist is base enough to go to life for his personages he should at least pretend that they are creations and not boast of them as copies.

The Decay of Lying

When a man acts he is a puppet. When he describes he is a poet.

Of a poet who wrote about a variety of subjects, from popular watering-places and universal providers to the immortality of the soul, he wrote:

We fear that he will never produce any real good work till he has made up his mind whether destiny intends him for a poet or for an advertising agent.

A romantic novel was dismissed with the remark that:

It could be read without any trouble and was probably written without any trouble also.

Shilling literature is always making demands on our credulity without ever appealing to our imagination.

The only form of fiction in which real characters do not seem out of place is history. In novels they are detestable.

The aim of most of our modern novelists seems to be, not to write good novels, but to write novels that will do good.

One should not be too severe on English novels: they are the only relaxation of the intellectually unemployed.

I write because it gives me the greatest possible artistic pleasure to write. If my work pleases the few I am gratified. If it does not, it causes me no pain. As for the mob, I have no desire to be a popular novelist. It is far too easy.

He admitted to Conan Doyle:

Between me and life there is a mist of words always. I throw probability out of the window for the sake of a phrase, and the chance of an epigram makes me desert truth. Still I do aim at making a work of art.

❀　　❀　　❀

He confided to Vincent O'Sullivan:

Now when I start a thing I must write desperately day and night till it is finished. Otherwise I should lose interest in it, and the first bus passing in the street would distract me from it.

❀　　❀　　❀

The basis of literary friendship is mixing the poisoned bowl.

❀　　❀　　❀

Lord Avebury had published his list of the Hundred Best Books, and at a function where the views of celebrities were being canvassed Wilde was requested to compile a list of his hundred favourites. He replied:

I fear that would be impossible.
'But why?' he was asked.
Because I have only written five.

❀ ❀ ❀

Writing about biography Wilde said:
Every great man nowadays has his disciples,
and it is usually Judas who writes his biography.

❀ ❀ ❀

The critic is he who can translate into another
manner of a new material his impression of beautiful things. The highest, as the lowest, form of
criticism is a mode of autobiography.

The Picture of Dorian Gray

❀ ❀ ❀

Formerly we used to canonise our heroes. The modern method is to vulgarise them. Cheap editions of great books may be delightful, but cheap editions of great men are absolutely detestable.

The Critic as Artist

The tears that we shed at a play are a type of the exquisite sterile emotions that it is the function of Art to awaken. We weep but we are not wounded. We grieve but our grief is not bitter.

The Critic as Artist

One man's poetry is another man's poison.

Books of poetry by young writers are usually promissory notes that are never met.

Medieval art is charming, but medieval emotions are out of date. One can use them in fiction, of course. But then the only things that one can use in fiction are the things that one has ceased to use in fact.

The Picture of Dorian Gray

A true artist takes no notice whatever of the public. The public to him are non-existent. He leaves that to the popular novelist.

The Soul of Man Under Socialism

Life and Living

To live is the rarest thing in the world. Most people exist, that is all.

The Soul of Man Under Socialism

❖　　❖　　❖

The first duty of life is to be as artificial as possible; what the second duty is, no one has yet discovered.

❖　　❖　　❖

A conversation with the actor Coquelin was recorded by Wilde himself:

'What is civilisation, M Wilde?'

'Love of beauty.'

'And what is beauty?'

'That which the bourgeois call ugly.'
'And what do the bourgeois call beautiful?'
'It does not exist.'

If there was less sympathy in the world there would be less trouble in the world.

An Ideal Husband

Nowadays to be intelligible is to be found out.

Lady Windertnere's Fan

Vulgarity and stupidity are two very vivid facts in modern life. One regrets them, naturally. But there they are.

The Soul of Man Under Socialism

It is pure unadulterated country life. They get up early because they have so much to do and go to bed early because they have so little to think about.

The Picture of Dorian Gray

❈ ❈ ❈

One should absorb the colour of life, but one should never remember its details. Details are always vulgar.

The Picture of Dorian Gray

❈ ❈ ❈

We live in an age that reads too much to be wise, and thinks too much to be beautiful.

The Picture of Dorian Gray

❈ ❈ ❈

I hope you don't think you have exhausted life ... When a man says that, one knows that life has exhausted him.

A Woman of No Importance

I never approve, or disapprove, of anything now. It is an absurd attitude to take towards life. We are not sent into the world to air our moral prejudices. I never take any notice of what common people say, and I never interfere with what charming people do.

The Picture of Dorian Gray

Life is much too important a thing ever to talk seriously about it.

Vera, or the Nihilists

Life ... is simply a *mauvais quart d'heure* made up of exquisite moments.

A Woman of No Importance

The world has been made by fools that wise men should live in it.

A Woman of No Importance

It is because Humanity has never known where it was going that it has been able to find its way.

The Critic as Artist

We can have in life but one great experience at best, and the secret of life is to reproduce that experiece as often as possible.

The Picture of Dorian Gray

I wrote when I did not know life; now that I do know the meaning of life, I have no more to write. Life cannot be written; life can only be lived.

In this world there are only two tragedies. One is not getting what one wants and the other is getting it.

Lady Windermere's Fan

People should not mistake the means of civilisation for the end. The steam engine and the telephone depend entirely for their value on the use to which they are put.

What seem to us bitter trials are often blessings in disguise.

The Importance of Being Earnest

If a man treats life artistically, his brain is in his heart.

The Picture of Dorian Gray

Definitions and Feelings

Caricature is the tribute mediocrity pays to genius.

To be premature is to be perfect.
Phrases and Philosophies for the Use of the Young

Education is an admirable thing, but it is well to remember from time to time that nothing that is worth knowing can be taught.

The Critic as Artist

In examinations the foolish ask questions that the wise cannot answer.

Phrases and Philosophies for the Use of the Young

To make a good salad is to be a brilliant diplomatist – the problem is entirely the same in both cases. To know exactly how much oil one must put with one's vinegar.

Vera, or The Nihilists

Nothing ages like happiness.

An Ideal Husband

Wisdom comes with winters.

A Florentine Tragedy

Moods don't last. It is their chief charm.

A Woman of No Importance

❈ ❈ ❈

A sensitive person is one who, because he has corns himself, always treads on other people's toes.

The Remarkable Rocket

❈ ❈ ❈

Experience is the name everyone gives to their mistakes.

Lady Windermere's Fan

❈ ❈ ❈

Industry is the root of all ugliness.
Phrases and Philosophies for the Use of the Young

❈ ❈ ❈

Seriousness is the only refuge of the shallow!

❈ ❈ ❈

Time is waste of money.
Phrases and Philosophies for the Use of the Young

The typical spendthrift is always giving away what he needs most.

Vera, or The Nihilists

Patriotism is the virtue of the vicious.

Moderation is a fatal thing. Nothing succeeds like excess.

A Woman of No Importance

Nothing looks so like innocence as an indiscretion.

Lord Arthur Savile's Crime

Ambition is the last refuge of the failure.

Phrases and Philosophies for the Use of the Young

Heaven is a despotism; I shall be at home there.

Vera, or The Nihilists

A sermon is a sorry sauce when you have nothing to eat it with.

The Duchess of Padua

Discontent is the first step in the progress of a man or a nation.

A Woman of No Importance

Missionaries, my dear! Don't you realise that missionaries are the divinely provided food for destitute and underfed cannibals? Whenever they are on the brink of starvation, Heaven in its infinite mercy sends them a nice plump missionary.

※　　※　　※

Memory is the diary that we all carry about with us.

The Importance of Being Earnest

※　　※　　※

A mask tells us more than a face.

Pen, Pencil and Poison

※　　※　　※

The well-bred contradict other people. The wise contradict themselves.

Phrases and Philosophies for the Use of the Young

Find expression for a sorrow, and it will become dear to you. Find expression for a joy, and you intensify its ecstasy.

The Critic as Artist

A cynic is a man who knows the price of everything and the value of nothing.

She who hesitates is won.

Ignorance is like a delicate exotic fruit; touch it and the bloom is gone.

A gentleman is one who never hurts anyone's feelings unintentionally.

Charity creates a multitude of sins.

Intentions

I have no ambition to be a popular hero, to be crowned with laurels one year and pelted with stones the next; I prefer dying peaceably in my own bed.

Vera, or The Nihilists

I don't like principles ... I prefer prejudices.

An Ideal Husband

I like hearing myself talk. It is one of my greatest pleasures. I often have long conversations all by myself, and I am so clever that sometimes I don't understand a single word of what I am saying.

The Remarkable Rocket

I like talking to a brick wall; it's the only thing in the world that never contradicts me.

Lady Windermere's Fan

I have never given adoration to anyone except myself.

I like to do all the talking myself. It saves time and prevents arguments.

The Remarkable Rocket

I usually say what I really think. A great mistake nowadays. It makes one so liable to be misunderstood.

I always pass on good advice. It is the only thing to do with it. It is never any use to oneself.

An Ideal Husband

I am always thinking about myself, and I expect everybody else to do the same. That is what is called sympathy.

The Remarkable Rocket

My duty as a gentleman has never interfered with my pleasures in the smallest degree.

The Importance of Being Earnest

I adore simple pleasures; they are the last refuge of the complex.

A Woman of No Importance

※　　　※　　　※

The most comfortable chair is the one I use myself when I have visitors.

An Ideal Husband

※　　　※　　　※

It is always nice to be expected and not to arrive.

An Ideal Husband

※　　　※　　　※

One should always play fairly – when one has the winning cards.

An Ideal Husband

※　　　※　　　※

I do not play cricket because it requires me to assume such indecent postures.

✦ ✦ ✦

I feel that football is all very well as a game for rough girls, but it is hardly suitable for delicate boys.

✦ ✦ ✦

I must decline your invitation due to a subsequent engagement.

✦ ✦ ✦

I do not approve of anything that tampers with natural ignorance.

... And
Impressions

Cultivated leisure is the aim of man.
The Soul of Man Under Socialism

The first step in aesthetic criticism is to realise one's own impressions.

Pen, Pencil and Poison

It is always a silly thing to give advice, but to give good advice is absolutely fatal.

Every effect that one produces gives one an enemy. To be popular one must be a mediocrity.

Tke Picture of Dorian Gray

There is a good deal to be said for blushing, if one can do it at the proper moment.

A Woman of No Importance

Good kings are the only dangerous enemies that modern democracy has.

Vera, or The Nihilists

Questions are never indiscreet. Answers sometimes are.

An Ideal Husband

It is always worth while asking a question, though it is not always worth while answering one.

An Ideal Husband

✦   ✦   ✦

The only reason, indeed, that excuses one for asking any questions is simple curiosity.

The Picture of Dorian Gray

✦   ✦   ✦

Lady Basildon: Ah! I hate being educated!
Mrs Marchmont: So do I. It puts one almost on a level with the commercial classes.

An Ideal Husband

✦   ✦   ✦

Everybody who is incapable of learning has taken to teaching – that is really what our enthusiasm for education has come to.

The Decay of Lying

Newspapers he suggested had degenerated:
They may now be absolutely relied upon.

The world is a stage, but the play is badly cast.
Lord Arthur Savile's Crime

To believe is very dull. To doubt is intensely engrossing. To be on the alert is to live; to be lulled into security is to die.

A truth ceases to be a truth when more than one person believes in it.

Phrases and Philosophies for the Use of the Young

We live in an age when unnecessary things are our only necessities.

It is only about the things that do not interest one that one can give an unbiased opinion; and this is no doubt the reason why an unbiased opinion is always valueless.

It is always an advantage not to have received a sound commercial education.

The Portrait of Mr WH

Duke: Have prudence in your dealings with the world. Be not too hasty; act on the second thought, first impulses are generally good.

The Duchess of Padua

A red rose is not selfish because it wants to be a red rose. It would be horribly selfish if it wanted all the other flowers in the garden to be both red and roses.

The Soul of Man Under Socialism

The Lords Temporal say nothing, the Lords Spiritual have nothing to say, and the House of Commons has nothing to say and says it.

Of what use is it to a man to travel sixty miles an hour? Is he any the better for it? Why, a fool can buy a railway ticket and travel sixty miles and hour. Is he any the less a fool?

The value of the telephone is the value of what two people have to say.

A thing is not necessarily true because a man dies for it.

The Portrait of Mr W H

Talking about public statues he said:

To see the frock-coat of the drawing-room done in bronze, or the double waistcoat perpetuated in marble, adds a new horror to death.

To do nothing at all is the most difficult thing in the world, the most difficult and the most intellectual.

Nothing can cure the soul but the senses, just as nothing can cure the senses but the soul.

The Picture of Dorian Gray

Those who see any difference between soul and body have neither.

Phrases and Philosophies for the Use of the Young

※　　※　　※

When one pays a visit it is for the purpose of wasting other people's time, not one's own.

An Ideal Husband

※　　※　　※

All beautiful things belong to the same age.

Pen, Pencil and Poison

※　　※　　※

There is only one thing in the world worse than being talked about, and that is not being talked about.

The Picture of Dorian Gray

※　　※　　※

To have been well brought up is a great drawback nowadays. It shuts one out from so much.

A Woman of No Importance

To get into the best society nowadays, one has either to feed people, amuse people, or shock people – that is all.

There is always more brass than brains in an aristocracy.

Vera, or The Nihilists

A cook and a diplomatist! An excellent parallel. If I had a son who was a fool I'd make him one or the other.

Vera, or The Nihilists

To make men Socialists is nothing, but to make Socialism human is a great thing.

To be natural is such a very difficult pose to keep up.

An Ideal Husband

The condition of perfection is idleness; the aim of perfection is youth.

Phrases and Philosophies for the Use of the Young

Philanthropy seems to me to have become simply the refuge of people who wish to annoy their fellow creatures.

An Ideal Husband

It is much more difficult to talk about a thing than to do it. In the sphere of actual life that is of course obvious. Anybody can make history. Only a great man can write it.

The Critic as Artist

The one duty we owe to history is to rewrite it.

The Critic as Artist

A bishop keeps on saying at the age of eighty what he was told to say when he was a boy of eighteen.

Arguments are to be avoided; they are always vulgar and often convincing.

Arguments are extremely vulgar, for everybody in good society holds exactly the same opinions.

❈　　❈　　❈

Cecily: When I see a spade I call it a spade.
Gwendolene: I am glad to say I have never seen a spade. It is obvious that our social spheres have been widely different.

The Importance of Being Earnest

❈　　❈　　❈

With an evening coat and a white tie, anybody, even a stockbroker, can gain a reputation for being civilised.

❈　　❈　　❈

Society produces rogues, and education makes one rogue cleverer than another.

Pleasures and Sorrows

No civilised man ever regrets a pleasure, and no uncivilised man ever knows what a pleasure is.

The Picture of Dorian Gray

❖　　❖　　❖

It is better to take pleasure in a rose than to put its root under a microscope.

❖　　❖　　❖

In court his habit of giving acquaintances cigarette cases was suggested as being 'expensive if indulged in indiscriminately'. Oscar replied:

Less expensive than giving jewelled garters to ladies.

The pleasure to me was being with those who are young, bright, happy, careless and free. I do not like the sensible and I do not like the old.

Musical people are so absurdly unreasonable. They always want one to be perfectly dumb at the very moment when one is longing to be absolutely deaf.

An Ideal Husband

I like Wagner's music better than anybody's. It is so loud that one can talk the whole time without people hearing what one says.

The Picture of Dorian Gray

Music makes one feel so romantic – at least it always got on one's nerves – which is the same thing nowadays.

A Woman of No Importance

If one plays good music people don't listen, and if one plays bad music people don't talk.

The Importance of Being Earnest

It is not good for one's morals to see bad acting.

The Picture of Dorian Gray

I love acting. It is so much more real than life.

The Picture of Dorian Gray

In her dealings with man Destiny never closes her accounts.

The Picture of Dorian Gray

The greatest sorrow of Wilde's life must have been The Trials. After them he wrote:

All trials are trials for one's life, and all sentences are sentences of death.

We are each our own devil, and we make this world our hell.

The Duchess of Padua

Death is not a God. He is only the servant of the Gods.

La Sainte Courtisane

Death and vulgarity are the only two facts in the nineteenth century that one cannot explain away.

The Picture of Dorian Gray

❖ ❖ ❖

One can survive everything nowadays except death.

❖ ❖ ❖

When told that his medical bill would be a large one he said:

Ah, well then, I suppose that I shall have to die as I lived – beyond my means.